Stories On Her Lips

Elise

For the ones who love stories...

Poetry, prose, stories

Our friendship with stories is magical
Stories will always be listened to
And we will always tell them

When we're young we are told stories.
And as we write our own stories, we tell
them too. Some stories, the ones that kiss
our hearts, stay with us forever. This book
is a home to the Stories On Her Lips. Her,
the girl who knew she was born to tell
stories, the girl who brings them to life
with a kiss. Explore the chapters of
Midnight, Honey and Kisses that are
filled with poetry, prose and stories. I
hope as you read these pages, you feel the
magic of the stories in your heart. After
all, stories are never just words, they're
the kisses life gives us and the kisses we
give back. So write your own story and
bring it to life with a kiss.

Midnight

Stories on her lips, stars in her eyes

Elise

She's the girl made of stardust and stories

She was both the fierce, unpredictable fire
and the dreamy, eternal starlight
the rarest girl in the world

Elise

She wrote her story in starlight ink
engraved in a golden tapestry
and with a kiss, brought it to life

She lives with the intensity of a lightning
strike,
alive and true
with wild eyes

Elise

Desire will never go out of fashion
igniting sparks and living with passion

I heard a story about a girl
who travelled at night to uncharted lands,
the stars guiding her way,
an eternal wanderer
searching for her heart in endless darkness

Elise

You were the poison I'd risk drinking
because I knew I could bring myself back to
life

The magic of the unknown is my drug of
choice
and I don't ever want to get sober

Elise

Come meet me under the stars
I will tell you a story

Burnt marshmallows on my tongue
nights like these belong to the young,
drinking memories so I'll never forget
under the stars, the night we met

Elise

Even in the deafening dark,
I could still hear the song
of your beating heart

The stories that ignite a fire in us,
the stories that make our blood run cold,
the stories that find a home in our hearts,
the stories that remind us why we are alive,
all start with a pen and a beating heart.

Elise

My earphones playing songs only I can hear,
behind my smile, hidden tears
I write my story, I choose my fate
you get what I'm saying, you can relate

And no matter what
we'll always be connected
by the stories in our hearts

Elise

Bitterly drinking our chosen poison
a promised escape into sweet oblivion
        ‑whiskey

I live for the moments my heart is beating so
fast
I can almost taste my own blood in my
mouth,
moments when I know I'm truly alive

Elise

The mischief in your smile
whispered that you wanted me
and the knowing in your eyes
said I'm the only one for you

Everyone wants to be a wild adventure on a
Wednesday,
well at least the ones worth knowing

Elise

Life's a game so play to win
I'm not backing out baby, I'm all in

My lust for you matched yours for me
we revelled in the escape we found in each
other,
bittersweet

Elise

Just me and my dreams
under the neon lights at half past three
high on the feeling,
my soul smiling back at me

He smelt like rebellion and tasted of home

Elise

On the stage, centre light
electric vibes, like fireflies
heart beats slow, young blood on fire
our voices singing, take us higher
midnight oil burning, we're glowing bright
you play that song for me, all through the
night
I felt so alive, potent and true
looking at them, I knew they felt it too

Adrenaline coated in sweet euphoria
let me feel this way forever

Elise

I jumped on the midnight express to the
stars
and ended up in your arms

There's something so undeniably magical
about writing stories from your heart,
stories only your voice can bring to life

Elise

The stars know all my dreams
I've got to keep going, got to believe
trust myself, no more pretend
as long as I've got me, I'll win in the end

We'll burn so bright the sky will set on fire
and we'll fly forever young
into the night that calls our names

Elise

Lyrics of my youth play in my mind
you and me, our love is the forever kind

The erotic way she'd bite her lip
and smile all at once,
that's when I knew a story
was coming to life in her mind

Elise

My heart grew wings
when the travelling art festival came to the
city
and put on their show,
painted faces, exotic scents
golden glitter on their skin
the living breathing artworks,
they created an atmosphere
where the lines of reality blurred
into the magic they performed.
I watched in wonder,
dreaming that one day
I'd run away with them
and live with the same magic
that they had abundantly in their hearts.

Stories On Her Lips

She's a living, breathing legend
leaving a trail of ink and stars
as she lives and writes the story of her life

Elise

Your voice took me to that somewhere place
between the dust of dreams and the pillars
of reality,
but with no golden thread to follow,
I had to find my own way back this time

Amrita, the scent of your perfume petals
when fire exists, don't you dare settle

Elise

Turquoise eyes
Aquarius star sign
Wet and wild
Dripping in mystery
Story in her smile
Her magic shines beautifully
Sexy body, powerful mind
Unpredictable, one of a kind
Desires a life that she can write
Sparkle like the stars, own the night

Going after a dream only you can see
means raising a glass and saying cheers to
yourself
with every small accomplishment

Elise

Just when you think you're close enough to
know me
you'll realise I've been playing at who I want
to be

She danced with her fire under the vast
desert sky,
the golden sands of time falling through her
fingers,
her white and scarlet dress shimmering
with stars
and with every heartbeat she thought only
of him

Elise

Highway to nowhere, I'll drive
wild nights with you, so alive
pizzas, pancakes, doughnuts and fries
endless adventures, that reckless gleam in
our eyes

When the show ends, take a bow
baby you're in my world now

Elise

I met a stranger at midnight,
but his scent of wild berries and burning
wood,
the iridescent golden glow in his eyes,
the scars on his body that intricately
matched with mine,
made me certain that we were not strangers
at all

I give my body to you willingly
but I'll never show you my heart,
the real intimacy

Elise

Honey, there's something in you I've never
seen before
your wild oasis and charismatic wit leaves
me wanting more

Bubblegum and gold cotton candy skies
your intense eyes burning me inside
sunset ignites as the waves kiss the shore
I'm feeling a way I've never felt before

Elise

I wrote your name in neon lights
a signal for you in your darkest night

Now I tug at my own heartstrings
my own muse, flying with gilded wings

Elise

Lurking between pages of books long
collecting dust
a labyrinth of legends waiting to be read out
loud
candlelight illuminated the chronicles one
by one
but the only story I wanted to hear was
yours

I longed for you to serenade me
with one more song from your memories

Elise

You were a dagger in the dark
I didn't see you coming
until you'd buried yourself deep in my heart

You always created 'forever moments' like it
was an art,
painting them with all the colours of your
raging fire

Elise

The girl with the heart of gold
she does as she wants, not as she's told
potent as lightning, lustrous like the stars
with her, it's 'come as you are'
plot twist in this story
the one I'm searching for is me

I was the architect of my own self-
destruction,
and I alone hold the power to rise from the
ashes
and create another masterpiece

Elise

We all have a wildly tumultuous
relationship with the night

The silence was loud that night
and then the fireflies...
the glowing embers singing so beautifully
in that moment I knew who I was going to
be

Elise

Your soul is your greatest work of art

The incandescent fire was a story before my
eyes,
the words consumed me as the wild flames
flew up into the sky
and I found the courage to dare speak your
name into the night,
giving wings to a story that I knew would
take flight

Elise

She winked at the midnight sky
and somehow I knew
the stars smiled back

Stories On Her Lips

Her wavy, gold-lacquered hair twirling
around her finger
her long, elegant legs that lead to her pot of
honey
her succulent, cherry lips bursting with
french kisses
her emerald eyes burnished with stars
her ravishing appearance was irresistible
but it was the deep beauty of her soul
that made her unequivocally an eternal star

Elise

These vivid dreams appear as stories,
alive and pulsing before my turquoise eyes

Sparkling nights in the eternal city
scent of dreamers drinking down the wine
they say all roads lead to Rome
but this one took me to you and you alone

Elise

She was the rebel that danced under
starlight
and lasted to see the sunrise

She'd dipped herself
into the ebony ink of midnight
and emerged with stories
like golden stars
painted all over her canvas

Elise

Battle scars and tattoos that drew too much
blood,
they all tell a story of who we are and what
we've done

Endless nights spent licking my wounds,
wondering if I'll ever belong
maybe I'm the last dreamer,
the only one

Elise

The swirl of storm clouds before lightning
strikes,
the skip of your heartbeat before you jump
into the unknown,
that restless buzz in the air before the music
starts,
the moment before the beginning of
everything.

She's got that turquoise fire in her veins

Elise

We were the only ones alive that night I
swear
driving down the highway to where no one's
gone before
we thought we were invincible
and in that moment, maybe we were

We sing songs to be who we really are,
somehow the music brings out the real in all
of us

Elise

My pink perfume smelt like wildflower
ruby lipstick and a short dress gives me
some power
men may think they gave it a name
but baby, women invented the game

Burning the midnight oil for you
writing our stories so they come true
words of brightest gold and deepest blue

Elise

I write my stories alone at midnight
but with the stars in the sky,
I feel my least lonely

The rebellious nature in us to go our own
way
bite down hard,
kiss,
lick,
enjoy the pain

Elise

Writing is mixing your blood with ink
so you can tell the story from your heart

It's like igniting the match you know will
spark a wildfire
that touch of destiny, your voice singing
with desire

Elise

I'll slip away the more you hold me tight
baby you're looking for sunshine
but I was born to the night

He was what I imagined
midnight to taste like

Elise

Stories come alive in the pure gloriousness
of the night

Stories On Her Lips

Her heart is in it
now she knows there is no limit

Elise

I'll write the lyrics for our electric love
and we'll sing the song with lightning on
our tongues

They call us reckless youth
but this is our time to be alive
to discover the ultimate truth
with the fire of forever in our eyes

Elise

Your invitation for a glass of red wine in a
Venetian bar,
was really a proposition that we intoxicate
ourselves
to the point we feel brave enough to rip each
other's clothes off.
But you didn't know that I had all the
courage I needed
when I saw the shimmer of desire in your
eyes.

Clouds of ideas and characters
swirling in my mind
you and me,
adventure and destiny
and when thunder cracks
and lightning strikes
I'm there, me and my story,
in the eye of the storm

Elise

So many stories in your eyes
so young at heart, yet so wise

She was the irresistible temptress,
with her forbidden treasure
that only some were courageous enough
to seek and find

Elise

We set out to live a momentous dream
but it was beyond our greatest imagination
what we would eventually achieve

"You could sail the seven seas and never find a treasure as rare as me"
-Elyse

Elise

The dream of her soul,
the golden rays in the inky depths,
sparkling forevermore

It was the wild beauty of her soul
that showed me
not all treasure is silver and gold

Elise

Will our song play on your lips or mine?

Stories On Her Lips

She will still be writing her story,
even if she has to use her own blood as ink

Elise

Storytellers,
those magical fire breathers of words
captivating hearts with their tales
making you believe in something more,
believe in yourself,
I'm going to run away
and become a storyteller

When it's so close you can almost taste it,
pucker your lips and take it

Elise

Why does this psychedelic feeling hit
when I pull you close and kiss your lips?

Live with the golden flames
and honeysuckle in your veins

Elise

I know you dreamt about me last night
because I could smell you on my pillow
when I woke up

Stories On Her Lips

She's like a midnight rabbit
that runs with the wild things
and a butterfly with golden fire
under her thunderous wings

Elise

Forever young, your beauty reigns pure and
true
it's your heart of gold
from legends old
that beckoned me to you

Stories On Her Lips

I drew an X over my heart
and you bit and kissed
and sucked and licked
until you made your mark

Elise

I'd wander along
forgotten roads at midnight
hoping I'd find you
somewhere under the stars

And you and I woke up
only to realise
we'd been dreaming the same dream

Elise

We rolled around in the midnight dust
until we were covered in the kisses
from midnight's lips

"I'll come back to hear stories about us,
as long as you're the one telling them"
  -Griffon

Elise

In all your glory
you stood before me,
you stole my breath
when you kissed my neck
biting and licking with your tongue
I felt the sweet pain of being young,
you stared at the bruises your kisses made
knowing in time they would fade,
so you gave to me a permanent mark
your kiss forever in my heart

Your glacé cherry blossom
intoxicated me all at once
and that's how I liked it

Elise

It was my heart that had been stolen
baby you're so fucking golden

One night with you
had me dripping with desire
in all the places I didn't know existed

Elise

Pull me close, hold on tight
touch my body, look me in my eyes
promise me now, stay alive

My heart belongs to my midnight dreams

Honey

Elise

I wandered through these melancholy
streets all night
I believed in the stories of once upon a time

Maybe we were always meant to live
the stories that we'd written in our hearts

Elise

In life's desert I became my own oasis

Drowning in a sea of stardust and memories,
deeper into the alluring darkness
I descended,
until a beam of light burst from my heart,
at the very moment I thought of you

Elise

She told me it was the oldest trap in the book,
she said 'don't be fooled, never grow up.'

Stories On Her Lips

All the birds and the bees
listened to her midnight stories
and saw the flicker in her eyes
that insatiable lust for life

Elise

The stars bring out her wild side
get ready for it and enjoy the ride

You will find no comfort from those
who don't understand the music of your
soul,
you're better off turning to yourself for
solace

Elise

We all have a story from our heart, here's
mine

Staying young is an act of rebellion
and I've always been a rebel

Elise

For me, writing is an ambrosian escape
into my own world of stars and dreams,
my own imagination runs wild
with all the stories alive in my heart

Alive in the place they sent us to die
throw us in the fire
but we've got the flames in our eyes

Elise

When I have low blood sugar
I run away to where I can breathe
toffee coated, chocolate strawberry air

Stories On Her Lips

I looked into your honey eyes
shimmering liquid gold,
and I saw a story of fire and fate and
friendship

Elise

We were floating in the aqua lagoon,
droplets like twinkling stars on our skin
your eyes glowing green
as you gazed into mine

There's no bigger adrenaline rush
than gazing into your forget-me-not eyes,
knowing what comes next

Elise

You locked your lips with mine
and threw away the key

Stories On Her Lips

You let me drink the delights
of that luscious nectar,
then tasted my lips
to experience the same ecstasy

Elise

Seeing his face,
reminded me of a story I once knew

I thought I was looking for you
but I was searching
for the lost parts of myself

Elise

I knew he had me
when I looked into those sapphire eyes
my heart was flying,
above the clouds in starlit skies

How beautiful it is to watch
the dust of dreams
daring to dance with the stars

Elise

Storytellers tell stories
that hit you like lightning
and strike a spark in you
that makes your heart beat again

A story I wrote for the stars
with every beat
of my aching heart

Elise

Pour that sweet honey in my ear
tell me the words I want to hear
you know you've got me with that ambrosia
fire
dreaming of us and those nights full of
desire

There's a story I keep closest to my heart
a story of me and my stars

Elise

Your name on my lips
felt like honey dripping into my heart

Stories On Her Lips

Drawn to the darkness in you
kiss my neck
taste me
fill me up with all the magic I see
when I look into your eyes

Elise

This golden age of legends and glory
every dreamer has their story

I knew it was you
when I heard the stars sing

Elise

.

We have golden soul ties
I knew it when I looked into your eyes

The only thing you risk losing is yourself,
everything else was never yours to keep

Elise

I kissed the stars goodnight
only to taste your honey lips
between the darkness

Nostalgic stories
always have a place in your heart

Elise

Playing renegades
with broken dreams and worn out hearts
but some of us aren't pretending

In the end all you've got left is you,
so make sure you know
who the fuck you are

Elise

The decadence and debauchery
in the twilight hours
couldn't conceal your tender heart

Stories On Her Lips

My turquoise fire ignites
across the endless sky
when you say the words,
look me in my eyes

Elise

Her lips were perfect
for pouring honey and stardust onto

Stories On Her Lips

She lives for the moments
when passion exceeds
the boundaries of morals
she calls them moments of fire

Elise

With the gold bonfire sparkles
I wrote your name into the ebony sky
only for it to disappear
after the sparks of our love burnt out

Stories On Her Lips

Lost in the shadows of night
I meet you under the neon lights
music loud, you drive to anywhere
honey scented perfume, flowers in my hair
I know you want my warm oasis
I feel so alive when we kiss
life's a song when we're together
I want to feel this way forever

Elise

It was a sweet story
you whispered into my ear,
but I was still gone before sunrise,
so I could write my own

He wanted the honey from my flower
and I wanted him to take it

Elise

One touch from you
ignites my very core alight,
we ride into darkness
with chariots of starlight,
as long as we're in each other's hearts
we'll burn bright,
golden fire
sprinkling stardust across the void of night

Stories On Her Lips

Spontaneous adventures
under starlight with you,
felt like antidotes to the poison
I'd been drinking my whole life

Elise

She is magic, the same magic as the stars

She was the girl with the golden smile
from the story he'd been dreaming about

Elise

Everything begins and ends
with a beating heart

Stories On Her Lips

You were all my nightmares
in one dreamy dalliance
of drunk decisions
and don't give a fuck attitude

Elise

She's the girl
the stars would watch in wonder,
dripping starlight onto her cherry lips,
so they too could be part of the stories
she whispered into the night

The stars told me a story last night
and then I dreamt it

Elise

Some stories turn your heart to ice
some stories make it catch fire

"It's on me this time."
"Darling, it's on you every time,
whether you know it or not."

Elise

Go where the fire in your heart burns wild
and free

Have the wisdom to be your own salvation
and the courage to act accordingly

Elise

And if I jump into the abyss,
will I come back the same?

Stories On Her Lips

Her name is Elyse
and believe me
she is as dreamy as the Elysian Fields

Elise

I looked him in the eyes
and whispered the words
he'd written in my heart centuries ago

Stories On Her Lips

A girl writing her story,
the one she breathes life into
with every beat of her heart
and stroke of her pen

Elise

She licks her honey lips,
syrupy nectar in starlight
and with her sweet tongue,
tells the stories of the night

Stories On Her Lips

Your nectar laced kiss
lingered like forever on my lips,
I suppose that was your way of promising
me
eventually you'd come back

Elise

You've got that liquid gold in your veins
unyielding and true, your eternal flame

Stories On Her Lips

Out of the smoky mist
emerged a lone figure,
she turned with tears in her eyes
to look at the howling night sky
and she wept and she smiled,
it was then I realised
she knew something that I did not

Elise

She wrote so many stories
it was inevitable
she would become one herself

Become your own home
and your story will live within you

Elise

And in the end
what are we
but the stories
we have in our hearts?

She told stories
like they were dreams
dipped in honey and starlight

Elise

I dare you to become
all that you know you can be
take the pen
and write your own story

Stories On Her Lips

Because the worth of gold
is nothing against the pureness of your soul

Elise

Hit me with that electricity bolt
watch me spark aflame,
alive in the dark
where the stars sing my name

She blew a kiss, tasty and sweet
with the scent of peaches and cream

Elise

If I descend into the pit of pain that screams
longer
you best believe I'll climb out stronger

You sang our song so it would come true
I knew in my heart it was always you

Elise

Our stories are woven in gold together
the legend of you and me will last forever

Stories On Her Lips

The nights charisma
brings out the lust in us all

Elise

"If I ever saw her again
I'd tell her how much she changed my life
for the better,
but I've got the strange feeling
that she already knows"

I've dreamt about you
in all the colours of my soul,
ours is the greatest love story ever told

Elise

Her favourite songs
are a roadmap to her soul

You pierced me deep like it was an art
and painted your love in my heart

Elise

She said the journey is the best part
but it's not meant for the faint of heart

In that moment
we knew it would never be the same
and our hearts beat as one
as we went up in flames

Elise

It was your voice
that breathed life into all my stories

Stories On Her Lips

He asked to join me
in that soft, sweet tone
but I knew this path
I must walk alone

Elise

I listened more closely
for the truth to pass your lips
when your words were wet with whiskey

Stories On Her Lips

When you're close to young people
you feel alive
because the fire in them
still burns wild and untamed

197

Elise

Go ahead, bet against me
I'll do it regardless, wait and see

Stories On Her Lips

"That strawberry shine on her lips
has me imagining all sorts of ways
I can make her my strawberry sundae"

Elise

With each story on my lips, my eyes shine
lost in the stars, I become so alive

Baby, is your heart still beating?

Elise

One last night immersed in Caribbean blue
drunk on the rum flavoured memory of you

Stories On Her Lips

I cry starlight tears
as I look back at the memories I see,
in my heart of hearts,
I'm glad I could share with you
this epic story

Elise

I'm drunk on the exquisite taste
of what it means to be young

I always remember
the noise my heart makes
when you look at me

Elise

And when you blew the smoke into my
mouth
I swear I felt a part of your soul flow into
mine

I was a shadow of myself in your world
so I ran away to be in my own

Elise

She is all the stars in her own night sky

Stories On Her Lips

We were at the edge of always
kissing lips with eternity
life's a dream or so they say
so I'll dream the stories I wrote for me

Elise

What's life without a little chaos
to remind us who the fuck we are?

We're the legends
in the stories you were told
when you cut us
we bleed gold

Elise

Baby I'm here for the epic music
of late night drives,
the rendezvous in highway motels,
the whispered conversations in diners
and the thrill of exploring
all the neon lights with you

We're out for scandalous times tonight
don't get in our way,
when the fire ignites and the music starts
you know the outcasts are out to play

Elise

Better to walk alone
and be able to dance under starlight
than to be false-heartedly loved
and never gaze upon the night sky

Stories On Her Lips

You can suck on honey coated chocolate,
lick sticky toffee apples,
press your lips into
sugar sprinkled candy-floss,
but baby
I'm the sweetest thing you'll ever taste

Elise

We were two kids against the world,
a story you've heard before
about a boy and a girl

Writing is in my blood
and so I write to stay alive

Elise

I had a feeling
she was the pot of gold
at the end of the rainbow

Be notorious,
the woman who lives
with fire in her heart
and stars in her eyes

Elise

Once those honey coated words
leave your lips,
there's no going back

Kisses

I've been strong for so long
I forgot to let myself breathe

Elise

They say Cleopatra
could seduce a man
with a single look
and I think to myself
how potent the mind of a woman
when she knows exactly what she wants

Even with everything you could give to me,
if I don't give all of who I am to myself
I'll still feel empty inside

Elise

It was the dream of love that we shared
the euphoria of stars
living in our minds

I've never been afraid of the storm
perhaps because I come alive in the chaos

Elise

Two lovers under the Mediterranean sun
pleasure and pain of being young,
dreamy waterfalls tempt us to midnight
dips
feed me with your love, a cherry pie kiss,
hugs in your arms that last forever
lips interlocked and souls bound together

Stories On Her Lips

I saw a girl with a denim jacket and blonde hair
looking at something that wasn't there,
writing stories in her blue book
stars in her eyes, one longing look,
ink and stardust all over her skin
imagination that never ends and never begins,
legends of a life gone by
tales told, magic she can look in the eye,
friends, lovers, enemies, they're all the same
quests and journeys share in the name,
her stories are alive tonight and forever
she lives them and writes them, sparkling together.

Elise

You tasted like Nirvana
and I craved your paradise

When a woman truly becomes herself
she ignites all the colours of her magic
the lyrics and melody of her song
the stars in her dreams
and becomes a fire
in which her story burns bright forever

Elise

The more I live my own life
the more I feel like that young girl
running barefoot through fairy forests
living and dreaming all at once

All he said when he saw her was:
"Finally, the reason for me living, has
arrived."

Elise

Once I started writing stories
I knew I would never stop

Passion amongst the stars
was our own euphoria,
stardust stained skin
and golden starlight
dripping from our lips

Elise

We made our bed in the stars
and revelled in the ecstasy,
your soul and mine,
that moment
was the only one that there ever was,
this feeling will always be mine

For such a girl
being alone is a part of who she is

Elise

You said we were sold on glory
I say we write our own story

I've got one last kiss on my lips
and it's meant for you

Elise

My lips kiss your Cupid's bow
and I feel a sweet pain in my heart,
I've been hit by Cupid's arrow
a love never torn apart

Stories On Her Lips

When her cherry lips parted for me
I saw in her mouth a glowing sea
of stars and stories

Elise

Glistening embers on her lips
you come alive with her kiss

Her stories are written in the stars
one kiss away from falling into your heart

Elise

I know most people prefer hugs
but there's a reason it's called a **kiss** of life

Even if my voice is shaking
I will still tell my story

Elise

With every breath from her mouth
I could hear the melodious song of her soul

Stories On Her Lips

I burnt the letters
I'd written for you
and figured
I'd let my kiss do the talking

Elise

"Her plump lips
   were the doors that would lead me
   into her treasure trove of stars
   and I was about ready to do
   whatever it took to prise them open"

Stories On Her Lips

Rhubarb and custard flavour gin
quickly passed my lips
leaning into you, your hands on my hips,
another long, sweet sip
before I turned to you and said,
kiss me now, in between my legs

Elise

Drink up the ginger and rum
and we'll live tonight
reckless and young

"I kissed her lips
and I could tell she craved
just once,
for a kiss to reach her heart"

Elise

One look into those starry eyes
and I was filled with all the stories
she'd lived,
one kiss on her honeyed lips
and I felt all the stories
she wanted to tell

Only your kiss
lets me breathe under water

Elise

I've left my lipstick kisses
all over our forbidden love

Her kiss left stardust on my lips
and the taste of nectar in my mouth

Elise

Kiss me truly,
in the beautiful chaos of shooting stars

Lost and found in the city of love
toasting champagne drinks under the stars
above,
feasting on pomegranates and plums
our hearts beating as loud as the drums,
I know you want to kiss me
life's waiting, who are we going to be?

Elise

I always thought that fairgrounds
are where dreams go to die,
but here, on this wheel, at the top
cherry between my lips, sucking on my
lollypop,
I wonder, maybe this is where dreams
need to go to feel alive.

And then she was gone,
the only trace of her that remained
were the rouge kisses on my skin

Elise

Everyone has that one song,
the lyrics are burnt into their mind
and the melody has a home in their heart

And I gazed into her starlit eyes
knowing these stories will last forever

Elise

She'd always keep one kiss for herself

When the scent of lotus oil is in the air
light a match

Elise

From one rebel to another
dreams do come true

I'm here to do nothing less
than set my heart on fire

Elise

She could call upon
that rare potency in herself,
like a Phoenix setting itself on fire
before it takes to the skies,
and oh how she loved to fly

You kissed me from dusk till dawn
and I awoke with violet bruises all over my
body
and a never-ending ache in my heart

Elise

We all have a kiss on our lips
that belongs only to one other person

It was the smell of burning wood
and lavender oil
that flooded my mind with memories of you
kissing my neck and singing in my ear
under the canopy of flowers and stars

Elise

Life is forever and fleeting,
come on baby, your heart is still beating

"That hidden kiss on your lips
looks ripe and ready to me."

Elise

It was the thirsty kiss on your lips
that gave you away

It was our first kiss
but your Italian cologne smelt like
those familiar memories
that are locked away in a dream

Elise

Never lose your lust for life,
for soon after you'll lose yourself

Those dark, firefly filled country roads
are where the hearts of the wild ones roam

Elise

With that one song,
the dream of life
becomes real
with every musical note

We were nocturnal creatures
who came alive in the story of the night

Elise

Stories are never just words,
they're the kisses life gives us
and the kisses we give back

"She told me all the stories she'd written in her book,
maybe I was their home now."

Elise

Snow covered January nights
a campfire in the woods,
blowing shadows of smoke
with every breath,
as we whisper all the stories
we were told to forget

She said:
"look up at the stars and you'll see a story."
 I told her:
 "the only stars I want to look into are the
ones in your eyes."

Elise

When you kissed me
I felt the stories of a thousand years
on your lips

Pink dusk
on that Hawaiian fire-lit beach,
we danced with strangers
and drank coconut cocktails,
kissing the oceans embrace

Elise

You kissed my heart
before you ever touched me

Losing sleep
because I'm wide awake
when I'm dreaming of you

Elise

Live with your passion dreamer,
fiercely alive,
pure vida

The weight of these words
is heavy on my heart,
still I will always speak them

Elise

Love shines in the hearts of those
who aren't afraid to know themselves

Noble young hearts
that love from midnight to noon
and all the way back again

Elise

She's the mystery
I wanted to spend forever
trying to solve

Maybe we're all a little broken
and searching for the lost parts of ourselves
amongst those eternal stars

Elise

Your kiss was the electric shock
that ignited the fire in my veins

It doesn't take an army,
it just takes you
and your relentless desire
to live your dream

Elise

Come closer
so I can taste your sugar coated lips,
you're like a California breeze
sweet but gone too soon

I knew I'd never have to be that girl again,
but I'd remember the lessons learnt forever

Elise

Driving down these country roads
singing in my white jeep,
my mind too wired on life to fall asleep,
one song is a kiss I'll show,
dreaming of you more than you know

I can't close my eyes
without seeing yours

Elise

It was a beautiful pain
when you cut my heart open
because it started beating for me again

From the hurt in your eyes
I could only imagine the scars on your heart
but still you dared to love

Elise

What is this lust that drives us to want
more?
That sweet, sultry desire for the legendary
Amor.

Forever I'll kiss the stories on my lips
and keep them alive in my heart

Elise

I took the sapphire blue of the sky
as a sign that you were near

The stories tell of a love
that survives time
and endures the distance
our souls travel,
I doubted if the stories were true
that was until I met you

Elise

These stories I've written in ink
have tasted my tears
too many times

Stories On Her Lips

I could feel the stories on her lips
when I tasted
her midnight honey kisses

Elise

She's the real thing
wrapped in a fairytale

I saw a sign that said:
'tell me a dream and I'll blow you a kiss,
tell me a story and you can kiss my lips.'

Elise

She's the story that lives in my heart
and haunts my dreams

I decided to stop in a countryside pub for
the night
I sat on a wooden chair by the whispering
fire
eating chips and drinking whiskey
writing my thoughts into a book
but as I wrote down the words in my head
it turned into a story all about you

Elise

1000 notebooks
would not have enough pages
to fill with all our adventures

I loved how
the stars in her eyes twinkled
while she was writing
a story from her heart

Elise

She gave me that rock and roll kiss
that lasts forever

I was born to write stories like these
– epic adventure

Elise

The story of the stars in her eyes
will live forever on her lips
    - beautiful smile

The essence of her story
comes from her heart of gold

Elise

The world is filled with stories
so how could we not have them inside us
too?

Tell me the story in your heart
and I'll tell you mine

Elise

Something about the look in her eyes
like she knew all the stories of the stars
and wanted to tell them

Maybe we're all living
different versions of the same story

Elise

Always with a book in her hand
stories on her cherry lips
stars in her turquoise eyes
and a fire in her beating heart

Even after all this time
your kiss never left my lips

Elise

I hear stories in the wind,
tales that have journeyed
from far away places,
legends that have found their way
to my doorstep
and I welcome them

Don't worry about what others think of you
it's only you who gets hurt
when you're not being all you can be

Elise

Kiss your story
and tell it to the stars

I wrote a story in the rain
and let the ink run down
all the way to my heart

Elise

Stories connect us all,
they're the stars in the darkness
we all look to
when we need to feel alive

She is drawn to those
whose story
beats loudest in their hearts

Elise

There's an old story here
a long-forgotten legend,
but sometimes
you can feel the tug
in broken hearts,
hear the song
in lovers breath,
see the sparks
in a warriors eyes,
and you know
one day,
that story
will come back to life

Run with the wild ones,
they know what it means
to truly be alive

Elise

Some stories,
the ones that kiss your heart
will stay with you forever,
they're the ones that are meant for you

Her eyes glistened with golden starlight,
it was like Nyx, the goddess of night
had created a human body
for her stars to live

Elise

These stories
showed me the world
in colours I'd never seen before

Stories On Her Lips

A song is a story with a melody,
but when it's her,
telling the stories on her lips,
I can hear
the sweetest music

Elise

My midnight girl,
I'll remember forever
the stories on her lips
the stars in her eyes
and the taste of honey when I kiss her

Thank you,

Elise

X

Printed in Great Britain
by Amazon

26981215R00188